Unveiled Beauty:
Handwritten Letters from a Poetic Heart

IS GIFTED TO

WITH LOVE FROM

DATE

PRAISE FOR UNVEILED BEAUTY

"Women from different cultures and walks of life all will find a story, an image, a truth that speaks to them. Lisa Harris offers a little something for everyone in Unveiled Beauty and does so with clarity, honesty and, of course, beauty."

~ CONTESSA BREWER, JOURNALIST AND TELEVISION HOST

"Unveiled Beauty truly embraces the everyday woman. By featuring ordinary diverse models, Harris captures the complexities and universal identities of women of all shapes and sizes."

~ DORRI MCWHORTER, CEO AT YWCA METROPOLITAN CHICAGO, WOMEN'S LEADERSHIP COUNCIL, COCHAIR AT UNITED WAY METROPOLITAN CHICAGO, MAYOR'S COMMISSION FOR A SAFER CHICAGO

"Lisa has found a unique way to showcase her passion for fashion, and the written word. She's truly created a heartfelt, multi-dimensional experience, and that's what true beauty is all about!"

~ ALLISON KAPLAN, SENIOR EDITOR OF SHOPPING & STYLE AT MPLS.ST.PAUL MAGAZINE, RADIO HOST AT SHOP GIRLS, MYTALK 107.1, FOUNDER AND EDITOR OF ALISHOPS.COM

"Unveiled Beauty is a gorgeous example of an internal examination of yourself while uniting women together through fashion, poetry, and personal passion."

~ LISA CASTRO GUTZMER, PRESIDENT AND OWNER OF CASTRO CREATIVE, FORMER DESIGN DIRECTOR, WOMEN'S APPAREL & ACCESSORIES AND DESIGN PARTNERSHIPS AT TARGET CORPORATION

"Unveiled Beauty is a beautiful collection of poetry. Each poem is as unique as the fashion that accompanies it. Among the pages of Unveiled Beauty, you are destined to find yourself, your mother, your sister, daughter and best friend in the words. Lisa Harris' insightful and intimate poems tell stories of love, fear, doubt, pain, strength, courage, and survival that will speak to your heart."

~ JASMINE BRETT STRINGER, AUTHOR OF SEIZE YOUR LIFE: HOW TO CARPE DIEM EVERY DAY, FOUNDER OF CARPE DIEM WITH JASMINE AND LIFESTYLE EXPERT

"Poetry juxtaposed with beautiful photographic images elevates Unveiled Beauty from a poetry book to a poetic odyssey. Lisa Harris invites you to tap into your innermost self with poems that send chills down your spine, tears to your eyes, and happiness in your heart."

~ KATIE CHIN, CELEBRITY CHEF AND AWARD-WINNING COOKBOOK AUTHOR

"Lisa Harris successfully combines three forms of art into one amazing work. Her method of creating Unveiled Beauty itself embraces her celebration of the intricate and multifaceted layers of womanhood. Unveiled Beauty will be a source of joy, reflection, and inspiration for many!"

~ VALERIE HILDEBRANDT WULF, SENIOR DIRECTOR OF DEVELOPMENT AT THE UNIVERSITY OF WISCONSIN FOUNDATION, DIRECTOR OF SALES AT MARY KAY, ATTORNEY AT LAW

UNVEILED
Beauty

Handwritten Stories
from a Poetic Heart

BY LISA HARRIS

Dear Lena n

Enjoy the journey
embrace the moments!

Carry on

brave warrior!

xoxo

ISBN: 978-1-945769-13-9
Library of Congress Catalog Number: 2016951791
Printed in the United States of America
First Printing: 2017
21 20 19 18 17   5 4 3 2 1

Cover and interior design by Emily Shaffer Rodvold at Lift Creative.

Wise Ink Creative Publishing
837 Glenwood Avenue
Minneapolis, MN 55405
wiseinkpub.com

To order, visit www.seattlebookcompany.com or call (734)-426-6248.
Reseller discounts available.

To Vanessa and Miles . . . May you journey through
life with an open mind and open heart. Dream big.
I saved all my stars for you.

Love you, forever

~Mama

Table of Contents

Praise for Unveiled Beauty ii	**Listen** 33	**X Chromosomes** 71, 72
Preface ix	**Delete Button** 35	**A Prayer** 75
Introduction xiii	**Dark Side of the Ocean** 37	**Mirror, Mirror on the Wall** 76
Morning Dew 1	**Risen Angel** 38	**Set My Heart Free** 78
His Eyes 3	**Opera Girl** 40	**Wake Up** 80
A Good Man 4	**Stars for You** 43, 44	**Purple and Blue** 83, 84
In God We Trust 7	**Perception or Reality** 47	**Welcome Home** 87
Porcelain Doll 9	**Milk Chocolate Kisses** 48	**Gracefully** 89
Solitary Confinement 10	**Insatiable** 51	**Laughter** 90
Reflection of Love 13, 14	**You and I** 53	**Our Dance** 93
Music in My Soul 16	**Blushing Bride** 55	**Hands of Time** 94
Words 18	**The Boxer** 57, 58	**Warrior Women** 97, 98
His Dark Princess 21	**Unanswered Questions** 61	*About Fashion Meets Poetry* 101
Shades of Brown 23, 24	**Thank You Card** 62	*Biographies* 103
Life in the Big Ten 27	**The Finish Line** 64	*Acknowledgements* 115
The Race 28	**Girl Walking around with My Heart** 67	*Credits* 119
Brick by Brick 30	**A Million Hearts** 69	

Preface

In your hands, you hold the poetry book I never knew I would write. For the both of us, this is the beginning—not the very beginning, but the beginning nonetheless. As I reflect over this journey, I'm fairly certain of the moment in time when this experience began, when something started brewing deep inside six years ago on a cold winter night in a lonely high-rise building well above the city lights.

It was one of those frigid nights where the wintry wind thrashes at your face, chilling you to the core. On that night, I didn't feel the coldness because I was sitting inside a warm building underneath the fluorescent lights. Looking around, the lights began to flicker as the janitor's footsteps turned the corner towards my cubicle. Sometimes, when I am alone in the office, that sound leaves an unsettling feeling in my stomach like an old Hitchcock movie, but not that night. The janitor on duty was someone I knew well. She was an older immigrant with a thick foreign accent that I had come to welcome on those late nights when it was just me and my computer screen. She greeted me as she emptied my daily garbage—the circular file that housed all my re-work, mistakes, and revised strategies.

I'm quite fond of this woman, and we knew each other by name. That is how I was raised; in many ways she is *my people*, or at least that is what my father would tell me as he began his drawn-out, animated story to remind me of where I came from. My father, a proud, simple man, only wanted his three daughters to respect their elders and never, ever forget their roots. I listened to my father's voice whispering in my head and acknowledged all the hourly workers by name, and in time, they came to know mine. On occasion, I was rewarded by seeing my grandfather's eyes or my grandmother's smile during those brief encounters in this overeducated building; I often wondered if these workers also journeyed to this country in hopes of earning enough money to send to their loved ones back home.

As a daughter of an immigrant mother from the Philippines and a Caucasian father with Native American roots, I was proud of the career I built in those four walls. However, on that cold night, I was reminded that I was more than the granddaughter of Filipino immigrants. I was more than my father's firstborn child. And still, I was more than an ambitious corporate workingwoman. I was a dedicated wife and a mother of two young children. As a businesswoman, I knew that a company was not obligated to ensure my success or my happiness. Their primary focus was on their ROI, and I was just one of many parts of a business model that yielded billions of dollars in annual revenue. However, after investing over a decade of my life to corporate America, the question remained: what about the woman, the mother? Did they know my son just celebrated his second birthday and that my daughter is a feisty four-year-old testing her independence and making her way through preschool? For the first time I began asking, *what about me?*

Sitting on the nineteenth floor in the taller of our two buildings, where hundreds of driven executives climbed the corporate jungle gym everyday, I felt alone. Lately, it seemed like every day, somewhere between my first cup of coffee and re-forecasting sales trends, I asked myself, why? Isn't this what I've always wanted—to be surrounded by talented people and to work for a company that prides itself on strategy and innovation? Isn't this the career that I've worked so hard to achieve in an industry I loved? Isn't it my responsibility to succeed not only for myself, but as a way to pay back my grandparents for all they sacrificed?

On this evening as I prepared for a forthcoming international trip, I missed the scent of my children and wondered what adventures they had been on today. I had enjoyed their bear hugs more than usual that morning and desperately did not want to leave them behind at day care. That feeling lingered all day in the stagnant office air and left me with a heavy heart, knowing that they would be fast asleep when I put my key in the door. Although I had a supportive husband, I had no intention of completely handing over the parenting reins to him or anyone else for that matter. All of these emotions hit me like an avalanche on this particular evening and began to snowball quickly over the course of a few short months. I slowly began focusing more on Lisa, the mother, and less on Lisa, the corporate businesswoman. It was the spring of 2010 and this moment complete with the emotions that continued to flood my heart were the catalysts that gave me the courage to walk away from that building—a difficult decision, but a crucial one, which eventually led me to the place I am now.

The next eighteen months didn't play out as I had anticipated, but quite frankly I am not certain what I expected. In the depths of my heart, I knew this change was necessary if I was to live a balanced life, but being a career Mom is all I had ever known. It was a label I wore with pride, front and center in flashing neon lights for the world to see. And now, here I was, empty-handed, without my business cards and fancy title, as I sat at home redecorating our house, taking care of the kids, lost and confused. I kept wondering, if I was no longer a businesswoman, who was I? Who would I become? And now, the next few chapters in life would test me and ultimately help to redefine me.

In sharing this time in my life with others, I discovered that those eighteen months birthed three important chapters, each with its own lessons.

Lesson Number One: Slow Down.
The first six months was a full release. Feeling freedom and a sense of relaxation that I had denied myself for years—a sabbatical, a mini-vacation, a time without deadlines and stressful meetings, a moment where I could actually appreciate the life around me.

Lesson Number Two: You Can Emerge from Darkness.
The next six months were some of the darkest moments—sleepwalking through my days wondering what I had done. I was no longer myself and had no idea who I had become. Towards the end of those six months, I couldn't bare the weight of sadness and I quietly searched for someone to save me. And then I realized, who better to save me than me?

Lesson Number Three: Truth and Knowledge Will Free You.
The last six months were a soul-searching journey that demanded I look in the mirror and ask tough questions. More importantly, it required I figure out what I wanted in a career, how to balance my family, and what I needed in order to be a healthier and happier Lisa.

After many internal debates, late-night glasses of wine, and networking with former colleagues, I made the choice to reenter corporate America, but this time I was doing it on my terms with flexibility and balance. Heading back to work was important to me; however, it was those eighteen months at home that changed me. Through that experience, a new Lisa emerged, or rather, I was reacquainted with my former self. This Lisa spoke to herself with kindness; her most beloved tools in life were her pen and paper, and she knew how to tap into her inner warrior to emerge stronger and more confident. This Lisa didn't require titles or labels to know who she was. In those eighteen months, I gifted myself something special, a gift that I had denied myself for more than thirteen years. I gave myself the gift of poetry.

In between redecorating the house, potty training my son, practicing the alphabet with my daughter, and starting a new job, I began writing poetry again. The funny thing is, as I sit here writing this very sentence, reading it, and saying it aloud, I can almost feel it breathing life right back into me. Like returning to your hometown or the warm embrace of an old friend, it simply felt *good.* This was the real me, a version of myself that had ceased to exist as the responsibilities of family and career had taken over my life.

Creative writing was a forgotten side of me, like the B-side of an old 45 vinyl record that the DJ neglects to play. What's amazing, even today, is how so few people have ever known this part of me—the writer, the poet. How could they? I rarely invited this side of me to the important events, and I failed to introduce her to some of the most important people. I, like the DJ, had abandoned the B-side of who I was.

Writing, like many art forms, can make an artist vulnerable in ways unparalleled in other careers. Whether it's a memoir or a fictional piece of work, the author's heart and mind are delicately woven throughout the composition, even when the story they're telling is not their own. The beauty is that, in its vulnerability, writing has the ability to heal. It became evident that writing poetry was as crucial to my happiness as leaving my well-established career had been. Reuniting with poetry, after years of soul-searching was like finding a vintage copy of *The Awakening* by Kate Chopin in the back of a dusty old bookstore, a treasure worth exploring. Breathing life back into the the writer within me was essential; I needed her and recognized her aching desire to be freed and to be heard. So I kept writing. Nothing could stop me. In this fragile transitional period, I found the key that unlocked the floodgates and the words poured out.

A journey that began late one night in a lonely high-rise building made another surprising turn as I approached my thirty-ninth birthday. For some women, heading into our forties is a milestone birthday that brings about a myriad of emotions and fears. Rather than address our fears head-on, we disguise them with antiaging potions before bedtime and frequent trips to the hair salon. Though age never bothered me much, I can certainly admit turning forty years old is not the same as standing in line outside the club on your twenty-first birthday. This was a different milestone, and I was a different woman. I found beauty in age and recognized for the first time that my bravery spoke in volumes I never experienced before. Bravery, along with the encouragement of a dear friend gave me the confidence to go beyond just writing poetry, but to share it with the world.

And that's how it all began . . . with unexpected twists and turns, a sprinkling of tears, and and a lot of soul searching; this corporate gal unleashed a poet. A journey that started at a crossroads in life and then lead me down the path of self-discovery and healing, to this place, this introduction, this book, the poetry book I never knew I would write. This is my B-side of that old vinyl 45 record, and I invite you and the DJ to play it, because it is definitely worth hearing.

Introduction

I declare myself neither a writer, nor a poet

Like my Native ancestors, sitting around a fire

Beyond the smoke filled air . . . I appear

Holding hands with a cast of characters

Re-enacting their story, re-imagining their pain

As the moonlight opens its arms,

A brave new warrior surfaces

I am more than a writer, more than a poet

I speak in your native tongue

Revealing the secrets of your heart

I am . . . a storyteller

Unveiled Beauty is not just my journey, it's our journey. Over the course of my life, I've had the honor of knowing, meeting, and reconnecting with compassionate, intelligent, and brave women. Collectively, we have walked through the hallways of depression, watched each other grow professionally, survived abuse, raised children, fell in and out of love, stood up to prejudice and injustice, encouraged and inspired each other and simply carried on. We carried on . . . together. With each story I heard, each article I read, and each woman I met, I fell in love. Yes, I fell in love with women, our raw and authentic vulnerabilities, our capacity to love, our ability to withstand hardship and heartache, and with the power of sisterhood, our strength to boldly persevere.

Unveiled Beauty is my gift to you. The women who grace the pages of this book represent all that is beautiful in women, each with unique stories and wounds of their own. But most importantly, they are your friends, your sisters, your mothers, your grandmothers and all the women in between. These women are you.

Unveiled Beauty is a reminder to you and a message to the world that our beauty has no boundaries and cannot be defined by media, unrealistic ideals, or the latest trend. Our beauty has no color and is seen and embraced in a multitude of shades all around the world. Our beauty has no size because what resides within us, in our souls, is boundless. I want you to see yourself, not the world's version of what you should look like. Not an untouchable, unattainable woman, but beauty that is present in the women we know, the women we are, and the women we love. Our beauty, the true essence of our womanhood, is celebrated in our minds, in our smiles, in our hearts, and in our tears.

Like you, I am beautifully flawed and human. I celebrate and embrace women; however, I have also hurt them. So in many ways, this book is an offering of peace and friendship to all women and serves as a celebration of all of us, all our beautiful differences, whole and broken places—the best and, sometimes, the not-so-good versions of who we can be. As a collective, we need to remember that we are more powerful when we stand together. As sisters, let's honor each other by walking graciously without judgment and reminding ourselves that each woman carries her own story of elegance, strength, beauty, and pain.

This book is not only about the inner and outer beauty that women possess, but it also explores our emotional journeys and the stories of our lives. These poems will undoubtedly stir emotions within you. My hope is that they make you think, they make you feel, they make you smile, and even at times make you mad. Most importantly, they are meant to keep you company and to remind you that whatever you are experiencing in life or whatever you have gone through, you are not alone. Sometimes we need to feel the pain and heartache in order to move past it, and sometimes, we need to get angry in order to redirect our paths. Regardless of what society tells us, as women, our emotions ARE our strength. This is what makes us women, and this is what makes us beautiful. These poems are a reminder that even at our lowest and weakest moments in life, we are beautiful—your sadness and brokenness is beautiful.

Today, six years later, I invite you to hold my hand and journey through these pages together. *Unveiled Beauty* will take you on a poetic odyssey through life and love. It's a secret dairy written from the hearts of women everywhere and a woman's anthem of struggle and strength. Somewhere within the pages of this book, I hope you recognize yourself, either in the woman staring back at you in the photographs or in the words that speak directly to your heart. These poems are not an autobiography of my life, but rather the moments in all of our lives. Some days I write from my own beating heart and other days I speak for those who cannot find their voice. So, whether you are reflecting on a difficult time, rediscovering your strength, or fondly reminiscing about the past, I want you to feel the warmth of my embrace and the comfort in the pages of this book. You are me and I am you, and I will not let you walk alone.

Morning

The morning dew kisses the silky petals of a single rose,
Clinging tightly through the daylight hours, unwilling to let go
Until finally, evaporation ends its existence

A rose this rare and elegant
Needs more than the morning dew that appears at the break of dawn
Solely to caress her petals and vanish into thin air

A rose this divine and fragrant
Requires the brilliance and warmth of the sunshine on her petals
And gentle rain showers to quench the thirsty soil beneath her roots

A rose this beautiful
Demands special care and attention to flourish and grow
Despite sharp thorns that may unexpectedly wound,
Her beauty shines from deep within
Expecting more than the other flowers in the garden

What this rose needs and what it desires are not always one and the same
As the evening hours draw near, she recalls what awaits her at dawn
Once again, she yearns for the kisses of the morning dew

HIS EYES

Affectionate
Not a child's, but a man's eyes
How they revealed his soul and loved more than I thought possible,
Those eyes showed strength and courage

Devoted
How could I disappoint the dreams in those eyes
And the road they saw in the distance?
Dreams I no longer had and a road I simply could not see

Sincere
They waited patiently for me but couldn't hide the sorrow
With those eyes, he trusted and believed
He not only opened his heart but also unlocked his soul

Without warning, the day came
That dreadful encounter when I had to face his eyes
After the painful words and shattered dreams, he stood tall
But his eyes, a man's eyes, reflected a deep pain
The kind of pain that only heartache can bring

If I forget every carefully chosen word I said
If I forget all the precious memories we shared
There is one thing I shall never forget
His eyes

The love of a good man
Like a soft blanket bundled tightly around you on a cold, wintry night
The warmest, safest place on earth to rest your head
He does not need to lasso the moon and all the stars in the midnight sky
For he has already given you all of his heart

His love is absolute, neither a mystery nor a fairy tale
Accompanying you through life without cross-examination or doubt
He loves you with steady conviction and unwavering truth
Prepared to weather any storm, for you are his lightness and his warmth

The love of a good man
Like the ocean waters that return again to meet the sandy beach
His heart knows its way back home
Faithful, his love does not wander the beachfront for buried treasure
For he has already found it: you are his devotion and his forever

His love is meant not to complete you, but to welcome you unconditionally
He is the answer to every question you have ever asked
And to every prayer you have ever prayed
He is truth, he is love

A Good Man

In God We Trust

With a microphone in his hand, he confidently stands
The soft chiming of church bells in the distance
Sharing a deep-rooted desire to lift up the broken and inspire the blessed
Mending the broken wings of God's angels on earth and drying their tears
The love of the Lord fills his heart because he believes
Like the loyal and unconditional love of a mother,
He embraces a faith large enough to accept all his imperfections and his greatness

Holding a glass of champagne
A designer scarf loose around his neck and an ever-so-dashing smile
Intelligent, complex, but with a hint of emptiness
In his faith, he trusts the inherent goodness in humanity, despite our wayward choices
Like a preacher, he strives to serve others
As a man, he lives to serve himself
Two worlds crashing head-on or living peacefully together

Captivating and driven
His eloquent words and thought-provoking questions stimulate the mind
In all his intellectual intrigue, he stands before her . . . a man
Enchanted by her presence and the beautiful complexities she carries
Lost in the moment, but always trusting that the Lord has a plan
Silently, he prays . . .

Porcelain Doll

Youthful, natural, and flawless beauty, a smooth baby face and feminine curves
Disguised as a grown woman, she tiptoes on the edge of adolescence
Beneath that subtle and sweet smile, she harbors within her a dark secret
Childhood stolen too soon, held for ransom at an enormous price
The price of her innocence

Apple pie sweetness unrecognizable now, a beautiful spirit abandoned her that day
Hiding behind designer shades of confidence, she's lost in a labyrinth of insecurities
Like the priceless antique vase in her mother's china cabinet, she protects her fragile beating heart
A trusting soul was violated that day, held hostage at a nonnegotiable price
The price of her self-esteem

Haunted by the memories that roam like uncaged animals in her mind
The horrific images pouncing and then escaping capture, she chooses to ignore the pain
Desperate to release the sadness that dwells within her heart
Slowly, this gentle, loving woman is taken captive at an unbearable price
The price of her heart

Guarded, isolated, and ashamed
Yearning to feel loved . . . Whispering to be heard
Begging to be seen . . . Afraid to be healed
This woman, this beauty, this tender soul paid a price that day

It is deathly dark and frigid in this dreadful place
Trapped, with no windows, not even a crack in the wall to let the light in
She's frightened, curled up and crying uncontrollably
She rocks herself gently to soothe her fears and calm her mind

In the darkness she can still feel his presence
In the dead silence she can hear his heavy breathing in her ear
The devil, he sits close besides her, laughing as she cries harder
He whispers, "I knew you would not betray me."
She grips the cross hanging from her neck and silently prays the Our Father
She does not remember inviting him in, and yet he sits there and laughs hysterically

It is only getting colder in this pitch-black place
She's terrified, but between her tears she gathers the courage to whisper in response,
"I was never yours. I belong to Him, Jesus Christ, my Savior . . ."
With a deep, low, and evil laugh, he says,
"Your Savior, do you think He likes this place?"
"Your Savior, do you think He is brave enough to sit in the darkness with me, ONLY to save you?"
Once again,
She sobs
She sobs
And sobs

It is extremely cold, and she is all alone in this frightful place
Gathering her strength, she rises to her knees
With her hands together in prayer, she begs for forgiveness and asks for His love
"I do not want to dance with the devil. Please save me from this darkness."
Tired, lonely, and afraid, she falls asleep waiting for her Savior

Reflection of Love

The road to love is not always a straight shot
The journey has many paths, unexpected detours, and dead ends
The road to love is not always crystal clear
It can be clouded by poor judgments, societal ideals, and selfish dreams

Love's youthful discovery can easily be tainted
We love in vain, mindful of what others will think of our choices
We look for perfection and commit for fear of loneliness
In our youth, we are romanced by love, sometimes without even knowing ourselves

As the years pass, we begin to see more clearly
We learn how to love and to be loved
We discover our true selves, what we truly desire and need
And sometimes, in this moment of discovery,
We realize that what's good may not be good enough
So where do we go from here?
Our youthful years are behind us, yet so much life still lies ahead

As life's responsibilities weigh heavily, we find ourselves at a crossroads
We are expected to sacrifice our selfish needs for those of others
We lack the youthful freedom to put ourselves first
The demands of everyday life have stolen that from us

The road to love is a mystery
Only you know the answers that will make you whole
The road to love is a story
Only you know how you want your story to be told

IN HER SOLITUDE,

she yearns to heal.

If she has to dust off the cobwebs

of her own heart and expose

herself to the world,

THEN SHE IS READY.

Music in My Soul

The notes linger like the smell of his cologne, dancing delicately in the air
They feel heavy on my eyelids
As I close my eyes, I begin to float
Lifting up my heart and slowly surrendering
My body moves to the rhythm—I am entranced
Their beauty caresses me over and over again

The lyrics are pure poetry in motion, laced with hidden meanings,
Dancing through my thoughts and challenging my mind
I begin to reflect
The words dive deep into the waters of my soul
Grabbing hold and speaking directly to my heart

Intertwined in a passionate tango,
The notes and lyrics hold each other close and then gently release
Without one another they are merely strangers in the night
Needing, yearning, desiring
Until they finally discover each other

In the midnight hours, I shall never sit alone
Like a devoted friend, the music keeps me company
Always present, always understanding,
The music bravely dances into my soul
As I grant it permission to access my heart

WORDS

Spoken, written, or sung
Captivating, they infiltrate her heart
In the womb she invented stories
In her mother's arms she listened to lullabies

Quotes, lyrics, and poetry
Bite-sized stories dazzle her imagination
Wrapping her mind around each one
In their presence she is spellbound

Words . . . so necessary, so desired
Pulling her closer or pushing her away
Verbs, they thrill her
Adjectives delight her
Adverbs intrigue her

Words . . . the heartbeat of the world
A multitude of roles they play
To expose the truth
To soften the heart
To quench the mind

In the depth of their meaning,
She celebrates life or drowns her sorrows
If only she could know and understand them all
Instead, she dresses them up in satin and lace or disguises them in black velvet
An abundance of words to choose from, and so many ways to decorate them
With all her choices, today she speaks with the beauty of simplicity

Thank you
I love you
Good-bye

His Dark Princess

Exotic woman, born in the tropical islands of the Philippines
The second oldest of four sisters and one adopted brother
The smartest and most determined of all her siblings
She dreamed that education would give her a better life
Like many Filipinas, she grew up in the poorest of situations
What most would consider the slums or the ghetto
Her story is one of hope and love

Hardworking man, born in a small Midwestern town
The son of a Native American mother and a Caucasian father
He spent boyhood summers on the reservations
Less than a quarter Native American, the locals still considered him an "Indian boy"
Early in life, he witnessed alcoholism and grieved the loss of a father he barely knew
All he wanted was to be loved and to raise a family of his own
His story is of loss and loneliness

Their story is not a traditional love story of its time
He was not a soldier stationed overseas
She was not a college graduate on a work visa
Rather, they fell in love through the art of writing and waiting patiently for letters
He once called her his dark princess
After marriage, he embraced her family and offered them a life they only could have dreamed about

This is only the beginning of a story
A marriage that would withstand love, betrayal, hardship, and sacrifice
His beacon, she taught him about family and loyalty
Her savior, he taught her about independence and strength

Shades of Brown

Chocolate, Mocha, and Brown Sugar
The color so exquisitely blended, untouched by the sun
Natural brown essence inherited from all those generations before
A flawless combination formulated by God, uniquely for you

Earthtone, Cinnamon, and Light Brown
The color desired by millions eager to possess the right shade
Artificial brown baked by the bulbs of a tanning booth or the rays of the sun
How blessed you are to wear that beautiful brown skin God created for you!

Caramel, Sepia, and Golden Beige
The color unfairly judged and mistreated throughout history
Demanding that you work harder alongside your fair-skinned friends in search of equality
Constantly proving yourself beyond the toasted brown skin, the skin God lovingly made for you

Bronze, Coffee, and Tan
The color of your skin, your hair, and your eyes
Natural brown beauty: after years of defying it, you finally embrace and accept it
There is no other color, no other shade that can match the beauty that you are

Shades of Brown . . .
Chocolate, Mocha, Brown Sugar,
Earthtone, Cinnamon, Light Brown,
Caramel, Sepia, Golden Beige,
Bronze, Coffee, and Tan
God created the perfect shade . . . Walk confidently in your beautiful brown skin

It wasn't the poetry, but the WORDS she fell in love with, and the characters she created in her mind.

LIFE IN THE BIG TEN

The girls are steppin' out tonight
Another Saturday night on campus, ready to impress
Young, pretty, and looking for fun
It's ten o'clock and the night has only just begun
Not concerned with what they've been told
Excited about what the night may hold
Nineteen years old, that was then
That was . . .
Life in the Big Ten

Walking up in that place and scanning the scene
Finding the perfect spot to settle in for the evening
Like so many other girls, she's waiting for him
After a big win, they know the boys will be celebratin'

Dancing with her girls and searching the crowd
She begins to worry that maybe he's not coming out
Lost in that thought, the boys arrive
Like last Saturday night, the place comes alive

Girls approach him one by one
As she rolls her eyes at all the attention
Respecting herself, she refuses to chase
Sitting there, she patiently waits
They only idolize his jersey, but that's not all that she sees
He's more than the hype, a young man of substance and mystery

Another Saturday night is coming to an end
He has been watching her all night; their eyes lock again
Unwilling to settle for one night in his arms
She expects a commitment, not just boyish charms
She's girlfriend material and makes it known
THIS girl is going home alone
So as she walks out the door to leave,
She turns to him and smiles sweetly
Nineteen years old, that was then
That was . . .
Life in the Big Ten

THE RACE

The wheels touched down
In a purple dress and sequined black heels, I was unprepared to run a race
And how was I to know what kind of race it would be?
100 meters, a 5k, a 10k, a relay?
To my surprise, it was not a high-adrenaline, fast-paced sprint
I found myself at the starting line of a marathon
Bib #011510

With no training and wearing sequined black heels, could I go the distance?
Was I truly about to venture into unknown territory?
Without knowing the answers
I ran anyway
I ran gracefully
I ran confidently
Bib #011510

Pacing myself, I enjoyed the first several miles
With the wind at my back, nothing could stop this woman in her sequined black heels
Then the race took an unforeseen turn down rough terrain
I cannot recall the mile marker at which the road became difficult, but it did
I pushed uphill, and at the moment of complete exhaustion
The finish line appeared in the distance
Bib #011510

The competitor in me intended to win
But, blistered in my sequined black heels, I had to make a decision
In that crucial moment, I chose to walk a couple of miles
It slowed me down, but my final destination was still in sight
Bib #011510

Brick by Brick

In her adolescence, she began to lay the foundation
Brick by brick she built it, sturdy and strong
With each disappointment and betrayal that wall became taller
Not visible to the naked eye, it stood between her and the rest of the world

It kept her safe for years—too many to count
There was no door, no lock, no key; the only way to reach her was to tear it down
And she was confident no one would have the patience to persevere
So she grew comfortable behind that wall, protected and secure . . . and happy

She was completely devoted; it had never let her down
That wall gave her strength and the power to face the world
She controlled who came in and how close, who stayed and who should leave
No one could ever hurt her again
It kept out the pain, but loneliness began to seep through the cracks

Years later, so many years later,
You came along and tore it down, that wall
Steadfast and patient, you wanted to know the woman behind it
And for some unexplainable reason, she needed you to know her and love her
So she watched as that wall came down, brick by brick . . . and she did nothing to stop you

Now she stands frightened and vulnerable,
Naked before you, with her heart in her hands
Should she begin to rebuild that wall, or is she brave enough to live without it?

List

I began to listen
Carefully . . .
Patiently . . .
Intensely . . .
To my heart

I listen because I've ignored it for too many years, demanding its silence
I listen because it's finally talking sense into my stubborn head, the place I always sought comfort
I listen because its natural beat has a new rhythm that is calling me home

I began to listen
Wonderfully . . .
Miraculously . . .
Courageously . . .
To my heart

I listen because I'm braver than I used to be and refuse to be shackled by my thoughts
I listen because falling in love gives me no choice but to hear it without distractions
I listen because it took years for someone to speak to it in a language it recognized

In its gentle and unassuming way, it tells me
Love passionately
Love loyally
Love deeply
It spoke to me, so I began to listen

DELETE BUTTON

Somewhere . . .

In a safe place, hidden away like a well-kept secret

He saved the photo book she created for him

A small reminder of the woman he once loved with explosive, volcanic passion

The delicious sound of her whispering "I love you" still rings in his ears

Like a favorite song played on repeat

As the months and years go by, every now and then, the memories of her flood his mind

Once upon a time, over a lifetime ago, in that fleeting moment . . . she was his

She can ignore his calls

She can delete his texts

She can block him

She can walk away without saying good-bye

But she can never erase the memories

Somewhere . . .

In the depths of her mind, hidden away like a well-kept secret . . .

She recalls that special birthday when he took her breath away

Standing at her door, offering a dozen fragrant red roses with a kiss

He declared "I love you" and time stood still

The sound of popping champagne still rings in her ears

In that moment, time was her friend and the possibility of love seemed endless

Once upon a time, over a lifetime ago, in that fleeting moment . . . he was hers

He can ignore her calls

He can delete her texts

He can block her

He can walk away without saying good-bye

But he can never erase the memories

Memories are all they have

The Dark Side of the Ocean

The sun was hot; the air was thick and humid
Swimming in the beautiful, majestic ocean for the very first time
Tasting the salty ocean waters on her sun-kissed lips
She's at peace as the warm water embraces her body

Uniting with long-lost relatives from her mother's homeland
She bonds with family whose faces she only recognizes from old family pictures
In a country she only knew from stories shared around the kitchen table
Warm familiarity of family sweetens the uncertainty of this foreign land
And then he touched her

Guilty, ashamed, and broken
Guilty, ashamed, and broken
GUILTY, ASHAMED, and BROKEN

In the aftermath, she was misguided
Desperate to keep the peace and afraid to disappoint her family
She locked the memories away, to surface only in her dreams
She dreamed and wept for months after, years after
Until there were no more tears left, and then every so often she'd cry again

This innocent girl became a woman
Making friends cautiously
Trusting only when necessary
Learning slowly, how to love, be loved, and forgive

So, to that young lady who still resides within her, I say this
Please, please, remember always
He had no right to steal your innocence
He had no right to break your spirit
He had no right to darken your heart
Please, please remember always
You are beautiful and worthy of love

The sun was hot that day, but it did not burn her heart
The air was thick and humid, but it did not suffocate her soul

Risen Angel

It was deathly dark and frigid in that dreadful place
The cold air engulfed her as she lay with her head on the ground
The sound of her tears and the overwhelming doubt in her heart were too painful to bear
It was time to save His precious angel

He sat close beside her, like a father bursting with love
He embraced her with a full heart
In the darkness, He filled the room with light
In the dead silence, He sang softly in her ear, "I am here."

As He cradled her face in his strong hands, He said,
"Dear child, do not be afraid. I will fight the devil to save you.
I will sit in every quiet corner, anywhere in this world, no matter how frigid, damp, or dark.
I fear nothing, and neither should you."

As He released her from her demons and forgave her, He spoke once more
"My love is unconditional. You are one of my angels on earth, and I will mend your wings.
If I cannot do it myself, I will have my most talented seamstress in heaven create a brand-new pair.
These new wings will sparkle with renewed beauty and the strength that only hardship brings.
I have great plans for you, and you need these to fly."

Opera Girl

A hush fills the room
Slow, soft music flirts with the air in the background
Holding their breath, the honored guests stop to stare
Whispers begin to flutter throughout the event
Like butterflies emerging from their cocoons
They cannot help but wonder,
Who is this captivating woman?

She crosses the room with flawless elegance, accompanied by a wink of confidence
A stunning navy blue strapless gown showcases her shoulder blades and makes love to her curves
Even the spectacular jeweled necklace that selfishly embraces her is bursting with envy
For it knows that nothing can outshine this woman's exquisite beauty

Although quiet, her contagious laughter ignites the room
Although slow, her touch turns strangers into old friends
Although gentle, her presence commands immediate attention
No man or woman could possibly take their eyes off her
A vision, a beauty, each guest privately craving to know her

The designer stilettos that kiss her toes are honored to escort her into the room,
For she carries an invisible, freshly polished crown upon her head
Tears from her past have dried, leaving peace and calmness to radiate from deep within her
Her crown sparkles with experience, kindness, and a newfound sense of wisdom
This is what they see, the radiance that casts a glorious spell all around her
They cannot help but wonder,
Who is this captivating woman?

Stars for You

In the deep midnight sky, they delicately hang—those stars
Proud and arrogant, it's no mystery why they own the night
They possess the secret hopes and dreams of millions around the world
How beautifully they twinkle; how brightly they shine—those stars
For centuries, they've left us breathless

In my youth, I wondrously
Gazed upon them
Wished upon them
Reached high for them
And dreamed

Wide-eyed and innocent, I captured every bright star within reach
Each a constant reminder of all I intended to achieve and all I aspired to be
And one by one, I faithfully tucked them away for safekeeping
Those stars, my stars, cherished and protected

Now I watch you, my sweet child
Staring up at the deep midnight sky
Gazing, wishing, reaching, and dreaming . . .

Those stars, my stars, I now give to you
Carefully pack them in your lunchbox each morning
Gently place them in your pockets throughout the day
And lovingly tuck them under your pillow each night

In the deep midnight sky, they delicately hang—those stars
Bold and beautiful, waiting to be captured by the next generation
As I gaze upon them with awe, I say to you, my sweet child,
Dream big
Reach high
And if you cannot capture all the stars you want, just reach deep into your pocket
And you shall find there all the shining stars you will ever need
These stars, my stars, I saved for you

Release the **beauty within** by the
power of your words,
the **tenderness** of your heart,
and the **depth of your soul.**

PERCEPTION OR REALITY

Who is he?

Dark skin, the color of molasses

Mysterious eyes deep as the infinite and turbulent seas

Dressed in a worn-out black hoodie and faded blue jeans

A brilliant Ivy League college boy jams to Jay Z's hip-hop beat

As he walks towards you, you quickly move to the other side of the street

Do you know her?

Jet-black hair with bright pink streaks

Piercing eyes, the shape of almonds, captivating those she sees

Dressed in a leather jacket, baby doll dress, and old workman boots

A well-read immigrant girl hesitates when she speaks broken English to you

As you exchange pleasantries, you talk slowly as if she were merely a child

Who is she?

Golden blonde hair and porcelain skin

Soft, charming eyes, the color of a cloudless summer sky

Dressed in a designer dress, carrying a Louis Vuitton handbag

A highly educated woman well versed in business and politics, with a friendly disposition

As you observe her, you limit conversation to small talk and the latest fashion

Do you know him?

Skin weathered by long days standing outside in the cold or the blistering sun

Kind yet hollowed eyes, as brave as the wild animals in the jungle

Dressed in dirty, torn clothes, he holds up a cardboard sign

A hardworking American jobless with no support system

As you shake your head in disgust, you refuse to look him in the eyes

Who are you to judge?

It is not the clothes they wear or the way they carry themselves

It is not the shape of their eyes or the color of their hair

Have we lost all sense of compassion?

These are God's children, our brothers and sisters

Only by looking past the surface can we know the person within

Milk Chocolate Kisses

White wine tears, lyrical lies, and milk chocolate kisses
Fresh, sweet strawberries, handpicked from the market
She feeds him
Addicted, high, drunk on the smell of her perfume—he cannot resist
So intense, so hypnotizing, the look in her eyes
Her face, her face . . . is
So beautiful

White wine tears, lyrical lies, and milk chocolate kisses
Candles lined up, too many to count, softly glowing in the dark
She loves him
Speechless, lost in the moment, he plays John Legend's song
Lyrics emerge from the darkness, filling the room, as tears fall from her eyes
Her face, her face . . . is
So mesmerizing

White wine tears, lyrical lies, and milk chocolate kisses
The moonlight peeks in around tightly drawn curtains
She dances with him
Dancing in circles of blazing reds and passionate pinks
Around and around they dance, learning as she goes; he refuses to let go
Her face, her face . . . is
So completely and utterly breathtaking

White wine tears . . . tipsy in love
Lyrical lies . . . blinded in love
Milk chocolate kisses . . .

Insatiable

Drawn to him like a hummingbird is drawn to the sweet nectar of a flower
To his aura, mysterious and complicated
An abandoned, broken man wearing a mask of fierce confidence

Like royalty, he indulges in her enchanted beauty
Taking all that is given without paying a price
On a fourteen-karat gold platter she serves him her insatiable love
Hungry, unable to curb his appetite, he sits on his throne
Overindulging in the flavor of sweet, old-fashioned vanilla ice cream

Fascinated by her, as a child is fascinated by the illusions at a magic show
Her allure, bewitching and captivating
A lonesome, bewildered woman hiding behind a dark, vintage birdcage veil

Like a wise servant, she knows his addiction goes beyond ice cream
Top-shelf Hennessey on his lips is sweeter and much more satisfying
Served in an expensive cognac glass stained with lipstick
The alcohol kisses his lips and burns his throat, leaving him intoxicated
Never satisfied with just one drink, still thirsty, he asks for more

YOU AND I

I desire
An embrace, long-lasting
The commitment of a promise ring
To share our hopes and dreams together
To experience love like this forever

I yearn
To kiss, so passionately
Your name next to mine for eternity
To lie with your body close to mine
To hold you like this until the end of time

I crave
A life, as your lover and friend
The security of knowing this will never end
To leave the past behind and begin a brand-new start
To know the truth that resonates deep within your heart

You are my one and only
No one can ever take your place
You are my one and only
Don't ever walk away

Blushing Bride

Lifting up her lace veil, she adores him
Visions of their future children dance blissfully in her head
Stoic and calm, he stands before her with deep admiration
After years of pursuit, she finally claims him as her own

Time, as it does, moves quietly forward, taking prisoners along the way
To the outside world she projects a happy home
Where the lawn is always mowed and the garden full of flowers
Privately, she lives a life of darkness, shackled by fear and denial

Once again, his convincing words replenish her confidence
A slave to her insecurities and the optimism that taints her vision of the truth
She clings to broken vows with a ring still on her finger
The echoes of promises wrapped in marital sheets

He loved her, he did, but he never tattooed her name on his heart
Still, he refuses to leave
Leading her to believe loyalty equals love
That he will forever be her rock, her refuge, and her peace
Yet, he leaves her alone in the dark—nothing but her tear-soaked pillow to keep her company

On a pedestal he stands, looking down on her as she weeps
She fears the light of truth will illuminate her weaknesses
Becoming nothing but a martyr, she relinquishes her power to keep their secrets safe
Lost and lonely, she begs to be restored

THE BOXER

It's Friday, and the events have begun
One by one the spectators begin to fill the arena
Anticipation of the unexpected makes her heart race as she steps into the ring
Sharp, beautiful, and strong, with a small frame, she stands

POW!
The first punch, straight to her head
The brutal hit shocks her system; her body shakes and her eyes water
She fights to stand upright, but it leaves her feeling dizzy
Like the migraines she often gets at night, her head throbs with excruciating pain
And she hears the crowd getting louder in her head, shouting her name and telling her to fight harder

POW! POW!
A strong left jab followed by a second right jab to her stomach, more intense than the first
Completely blindsided, she is astonished; how could she not see this coming?
Leaning on the ropes, trying to catch her breath, body trembling and gasping for air
She bends over, feeling sick to her stomach, and knows she will not be able to eat for days
And, in her head, she hears the crowd roaring with excitement, telling her to stay the course

POW!

The last deadly punch directly to her chest

Like a knife straight through her heart, she feels a pain so unbearable, she finally begins to cry

Shaking once again, uncontrollably now, her knees weaken

In her disbelief, she cannot decipher the lies and deceit that left her so weak

And in her head, one last time, she hears the crowd shouting in anger to give up the fight

1 . . . 2 . . . 3 . . . 4 . . . Knockout!

Her beautiful, strong, small frame falls hard to the floor

Sweating, sobbing as mascara-stained tears fall down her cheeks

Down she goes in a pool of blood

From her bleeding heart

Finally, the crowds are silent in her head

SHE MISTAKENLY SMELLED

honesty

WHEN HE STILL HAD

betrayal

ON HIS BREATHE.

Unanswered Questions

If she knew then what she knows now
Would she have opened her heart so freely?
Innocently trusting everyone before doubting a single soul . . .
If she knew then what she knows now
Would she have embraced love so completely?
Innocently giving all she had to give . . .
If she knew then what she knows now
Would she have listened so faithfully?
Innocently believing everyone spoke from the heart . . .

But back then, she thought with her heart
She called,
She waited,
She dreamed,
And astonishingly, she loved
She loved so purely and so completely
If she knew then what she knows now . . .

Now is Now . . .
And there are days when she wishes she never knew at all . . .
Simply stated, life has taught her
Now she doubts everyone before trusting a single soul
Now she walks bravely with her eyes wide open, but her heart closed
Because now she knows
Now she can hardly open the heart that once was so free
She's no longer as innocent as she used to be
And now I ask,
If she knew then what she knows now
Would she have loved any differently?

Thank You Card

With determination and love, she stood firm beside me like a beautiful statue
Just like those ancient sculptures scattered across Europe's small, forgotten towns
Battles and storms left them broken and weathered, but still they stand tall
As she stood for years, without fail, right by my side

No foolish word or wayward choice could turn her away; she never opened the door to leave
No outrageous story or wasted tears could alter her love; she never packed her suitcase
In those moments when I felt isolated and detached from the world, she never stopped calling
In the height of the storm, with dark, thunderous clouds overhead, she never abandoned me

She listened
She counseled
She prayed

Like a loyal housekeeper, she arrived every day, on time
To sweep up the shattered glass
Wiping away my tears with the sincerity of her words
Dusting away the cobwebs of insecurity spun around me
Never expecting anything in return

"Don't give up on me," I said time and time again
Quietly begging, pleading, and praying
She strode into my heart without judgment
Caring for me in all the ways I needed to make it through this journey
Reminding me of my worth and inner beauty when I was too blinded to see
She said, "I will not give up on you."
She never did

THE FINISH LINE

Wearing my sequined black heels, I simply could not compete with her
The woman wearing the bright blue running shoes
She came swiftly from behind and passed me in the final stretch
She had the advantage from the very start
She trained harder, she steadied her pace, and she never stopped
This clearly was not my race to win; a different race awaits me
So, today, I trade in my sequined black heels
For a brand-new pair of bright pink running shoes
Bib #011510

Girl Walking around with My Heart

Here she comes to face the day
Dressed in a graphic shirt and a pink polka-dot tulle skirt
Wearing turquoise-and-hot-pink leopard-print socks
Joyfully skipping down the stairs, bright-eyed, curious, and full of life

With a smile, I say, "Have you brushed your hair today?"
A beautiful, light brown tangled mess as wild and free as her spirit
Crossing her arms, she replies, "Why does everything have to be so perfect?"
At eleven years old, this girl is as fiery and sassy as her mother
There she goes, walking around with my heart

There she goes off to face the world
Intelligent and empathetic, with a million questions
Who are angels, Mama?
Why did the corner store go out of business?
If I pray for Daddy, will he hear me?
Today she is destined to save endangered panda bears
Tomorrow she dreams of becoming an Olympic gymnast

Oh, how I adore her pure innocence and zest for life
My beautiful girl, my friend for life, my heart, my love
Wearing her emoji shirt with glitter, a crochet vest, and a light pink skirt
There she goes, walking around with my heart

A Million Hearts

Pink trees dripping with diamonds surround her as she tiptoes down a mysterious path
A mystical place untouched by darkness, where the lonely hearts are forbidden
As her curiosity unfolds, she eases forward only to reach a clearing . . .
Gasping with sheer surprise
Not a cloud in sight, only the most spectacular bright blue sky
Peace, truth, and love pour over her
Running barefoot through the grass with wonderment, the fairy dust tickling her toes

Gently untying a bow and unwrapping her heart, she gives it permission to fly
Like white doves released at a wedding, her heart embraces the freedom of the open sky
With her face turned towards the sun, she is enchanted by the beauty around her
In that magical moment, a million hearts fall from the sky
Showering down on her in abundance, like an explosion of confetti
An array of colorful pink sensation delights her heart

Magenta, Fuchsia, Carnation Pink,
Rose, Cerise, Hot Pink, and Mauve
A million hearts fall from the sky

Bursting with joy in their company
Raising her arms towards the bright blue sky, she twirls like a child
Broken, beautiful, and brave
Full of hope
Full of life
Full of love
One by one they fall
A million hearts from the sky

X CHROMOSOMES

The female body, so exquisitely made, with its natural, God-given curves
A masterpiece recreated for centuries in statues and paintings all over the world
We are constantly reminded to respect it and protect it
Without the female body, human life is simply nonexistent
Yet movies, music, and magazines continue to disrespect and objectify it
What shall we believe?
My X chromosomes and me

The female mind, intricately woven with intellect, compassion, and curiosity
Our sisters in the feminist movement fought for equality so our voices could be free
Today, generations later, brilliant women assemble in lecture halls at the finest universities
As breadwinners, we sit at the head of the family dinner table
Yet America continues to devalue our contributions and robs us of our equal pay
What shall we believe?
My X chromosomes and me

The female heart, vast and deep as the majestic oceans
We cradle a baby in one arm and hold a lover's hand with the other
Unafraid to carry our hearts into the boardroom, we still make the tough decisions
As active community leaders, we boldly create a better world for the next generation
Yet society continues to declare our emotions are our weakness
What shall we believe?
My X chromosomes and me

Let your voice be heard, watch what you say
Love your body, lose some weight
Be independent, serve your man

My X chromosomes and me

We will
     Be the next president
          Stay home to raise happy children
     Discover the cure for cancer

We will
Write a best-selling novel
Dance on the bar
Win an Olympic gold medal

We will . . . My X chromosomes and me

Searching for bible verses in the stars and counting blessings like teardrops amongst the constellations.

A Prayer

Stillness in the night
A silent, soft buzzing in the distance accompanies the midnight quiet
With clean, crisp white sheets pulled close around him, he drifts into a deep sleep
Lost in his dreams, he journeys to a hidden place, where his heart, mind, and body feel free . . .

Stillness in the night
She watches him sleep
The slow and rhythmic motion of each breath he quietly takes in and out
Sleeping peacefully with the turbulence of the day's events soon behind him
The deep lines that map his face during the day have finally disappeared
In his moment of quiet solitude, he knows not that she still watches him with love

Stillness in the night
She knows he doubts her love
The tender warmth of her embrace a mere memory locked away in the closets of his mind
Like a ghost it haunts him in the daylight hours, and she wonders, will he ever hold her again?
Sad beyond words, she knows he needs her to fill the emptiness in his heart
In his moment of peaceful rest, he knows not that she still watches him with love

Stillness in the night
She desperately searches for the path that will lead her back to him
He is irreplaceable
With every ounce of her being, she must find a way to fall in love with him again
For now, she watches him . . .

Mirror, Mirror on the Wall

With a condescending smile, she says,
"Look at yourself in the mirror.
How can you call yourself a real woman?"

How dare YOU command ME to look in the mirror?
I recognize the woman staring back at me
Despite her shortcomings, she is a woman worth knowing
She is my loyal and faithful friend
I know her well

She is a real woman, not fabricated or false
And when I look in the mirror, it is a real woman I see
Confident and insecure
Courageous and weak
Honest and deceitful

She is a real woman, not fantasy or fiction
And when I look in the mirror, it is a real woman I see
Selfless and selfish
Kind and hurtful
Brilliant and naive

How dare YOU command ME to look in the mirror?
I do not claim to stand before you perfect, and I do not expect you to understand me
But do not judge my actions or pretend to know the workings of my heart
I live and breathe, laugh and cry, just like you
I AM a real woman

How dare YOU command ME to look in the mirror?
With compassion, I ask you . . . when YOU look in the mirror
Who do YOU see?

Set My Heart Free

He walked into her life
When her life no longer had meaning
He danced into her heart
When her heart had stopped beating

Before he came along
She stopped believing
She stopped loving
And she stopped living

He waltzed into her life
And set her heart free
With the gift of his love
Her heart can now breathe

WAKE UP

With a roar so courageous and loud
It shakes the kingdom with raw, emotional intensity,
Her blood boils up inside at 212 degrees Fahrenheit,
And she erupts with wicked words
You are the coward
You are the fool
You are the consolation prize

Playing the jester and servant to your king
While he winks at his ladies-in-waiting and beams with delight
Feeding him your never-ending love with a silver spoon
While he laughs at your jokes then plays you the fool

Wake up! Don't you see?
You are not his beloved
You are not his confidant
You are not his queen

Rise up from your knees and stop worshiping this man
He's playing a game, and he'll never show you his hand
His loyalty is feigned, and you freely drink from his cup
Everyone is laughing ...
I beg you, please wake up!

With a thunderous voice that carries through time
She shouts with conviction to all the ladies in denial
Don't be the coward
Don't be the fool
Don't be the consolation prize

Purple

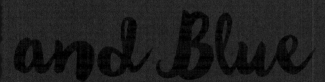
and Blue

Look at me
Look at me
Stop for a moment and look at me

Trembling on the witness stand, I bravely set my right hand on the Bible
"I swear to tell the truth, the whole truth, and nothing but the truth, so help me God."
Like a fast pitch in Major League Baseball, you fire the questions at me
Hitting me harder than that very first time he did
You stand there, self-righteous, overeducated, in your designer suit
Arrogantly believing you would never let a man treat you the way he treats me
The interrogation unfolds …
WHY?
WHY?

Look at me
Look at me
Stop for a moment and look at me

My battered face is beautiful behind the shades of purple and blue
My eyes, now half shut and swollen, once sparkled with pure happiness
My bruised and broken heart once believed true love could conquer all
My mind, now distracted by daily migraines, is brilliant just like yours

Yes, he hit me, beat me, and left me there to weep
Yes, he cheated on me for years, speaking well-crafted lies
Yes, he abused me, physically, emotionally, and mentally
Yes, I stayed

Sitting beside the judge with shaking knees, I boldly turned towards the jury
"He loves me."
"He promised it would never happen again."
With curious eyes, my peers simply stared at me
Piercing right through me, past my self-convincing words, straight to my heart
You sit there astonished, noticeably confused with pity drawn on your face
Confident that you would never stay with a man like mine
The interrogation continues ...
WHY?
WHY?

Tears well up in my eyes.
How could you possibly understand our love?
The man who counted every star in the evening sky for me
The man who believed in me as I chased my dreams
The man who complimented me often with such adoring words
The man who proposed on one knee and promised before God to honor me in
good times and bad
The man who held our newborn in his arms
You were not there . . . He was

This troubled man was my everything
I was going to save him
Our love would prevail

Then he hit me again

Bathing in a shower of love.

Water gently pours down her body,

washing all the sadness from her skin.

A reminder she must first

love herself.

Welcome Home

An unexpected knocking on the door startles me
The raging waters of anxiety rush through my body
A quickening of my heartbeat strangles my breathing
Uncertain about the mystery that waits on the other side

I cautiously unlock the door . . . there stands a woman
Magnificent as a portrait I once saw in a world-renowned art gallery in Rome
Her mere presence overwhelms me
She's fearlessly confident; any insecurity in her is unrecognizable
A pillar of strength and beauty, no sign of dependency or vulnerability
No, not her
This woman stood there, in all her glory, her most dignified and best self

A slow sigh of pure relief extinguishes all my fears and anxieties
Without hesitation, she extends her arms in an offering of friendship and peace
The warmth of her embrace floods my mind with an myriad of memories
Memories of her . . . this woman
Oh, how I loved her
Oh, how I idolized her
Oh, how I've missed her
I never imagined I would abandon her . . . this woman

As our eyes meet, she knows I recognize her and finally beams with pride
There is a softness and gentleness in her eyes, as though she observes a child
She knows my journey as if it was her own, her own life lessons
I look into her eyes, my eyes, and I welcome her home

Gracefully

Watch . . . as I walk away
Gracefully

Refusing to stand in the thick quicksand beneath my feet
Sinking deeper and deeper into a life of loneliness
Foolishly walking blindfolded through the deceptions of love

Packing up the memories, folding them neatly, and simply moving on
Gently returning to you the shirt, the toothbrush, and the ingenious web of lies
Emerging from the darkness, freed by the truth

Watch . . . as I walk away
Gracefully

Laughter

It's loud and fantastic
Laughter always makes a grand entrance
Jumping, dancing, and moving like lightning through space and time
Not intended to be stifled or to drift slowly, like a whisper floating into thin air
It makes our hearts overflow with joy as it kisses all those around us

The sound skips through the air, tickling our eardrums with delight
Hearing its melody fills our souls to the brim with sweetness
It hypnotizes us in its magical presence; we are entranced
Until our bodies can no longer stand still and we too surrender to its charm

It's loud and fantastic
Laughter always makes a grand entrance
Leaping, prancing, singing like children in unison on a carousel ride
It has a deep friendship with the smile and will not succumb to the frown
Laughter . . . so beautiful, so precious,
If only we could hold on to it for a little while longer

Our Dance

May I have this dance?

I extend my hand

His tender smile tugs at my heart as his small hand reaches for mine

Breathing in his little-boy scent, I hold him close, as though it's necessary for my survival

Embracing him awakens memories of the first time we met

That cold, snowy day in February when our hearts were intertwined

Adoringly, he gazes up at me

"I love you, Mama."

Until every last star in heaven burns out, you will be mine

My heart, my love, my little man

The days pass, the weeks, the months, the years . . .

Moving slowly like the glaciers that created our beautiful Great Lakes

Or at times moving with the force and speed of a Colorado avalanche

In my quiet moments, I reminisce about

Early morning kisses on his boyish bedhead as he climbs into my lap

Sunny afternoons watching him play football in the neighborhood park

Late-night bedtime stories followed by Mama's kisses and cuddles

All cherished memories tucked away in a baby book in my mind

May I have this dance?

He extends his hand

With tears flowing down my beautifully aged face, I desperately take it

Wondering how I allowed time to slip away, my heart breaks as he wipes away my tears

Wishing this handsome man who holds me now was still small enough to cuddle and kiss goodnight

In that moment, my heart refuses to let him go

Standing there in his tuxedo, he looks deep into my eyes

"I love you, Mama."

Until all the stars in heaven burn out, you will be mine

My heart, my love, my little man

All eyes on us, as the DJ plays our song

Then I feel a tap on my shoulder

And she says,

May have this dance?

HANDS OF TIME

The years glide elegantly across the stage of our lives
Our feet barely touch the ground as we move through time
When we close our eyes, blurred memories and forgotten dreams dance by

A woman
Stands before her honest and faithful mirror in the shadows of her bedroom
How beautifully the laugh lines etch each side of her mouth
Sitting in quiet company with delicate wrinkles at the edges of her deep brown eyes

Together, they reminiscence about youthful days, a time before they mapped her face
Long summer nights that warmed her heart with bonfire kisses and innocent love
Carefree days filled with spontaneous adventures and high-speed carnival rides

A woman
Gazes intently into her trusting and loyal mirror in the corner of her dressing room
Her reflection, no matter how breathtaking, is inconsistent with the youthful face she sees in her mind
Looking into the eyes of an older woman, she still cradles a romantic heart full of hopes and dreams

Hands like her mother's reveal her age
Silver highlights play hide and seek in her long brown hair
Dark circles paint a shadowy hue below her tired eyes

The years lead us in this dance through time
Guiding us into the future with renewed wisdom and strength
Each year welcoming new dancers and choreographing new steps

Older, wiser, and more beautiful than ever before
A dance, a woman, a life . . .
Together, the way they move, the way they live, the way they love
Deserves nothing less than a standing ovation

Warrior Women

Gathering berries, with her newborn strapped close to her chest
Breathing in the fresh autumn air of the Northwoods
And feeling her baby's heartbeat in rhythm with her own,
Off in the distance, she hears the beating of the ceremonial drums calling her name
Raped by the new settler disguised as a friend
Violated, betrayed, and left behind
Stripped of her land, where her heart lies buried deep within the rich soil
Be Zha Ge Zha Geh Kwe, daughter of Ojibwa Nation . . .
Carry on, brave warrior

Sweating from the hot, Mississippi sun, with blistering hands and feet
Picking cotton for hours in the vast cotton fields of the South
Passing her time and pacing her work, she sings in harmony with her sisters
They sing of hope and despair, their voices reach high towards the sun
Beaten and whipped at the hands of her master
Frightened, furious, and dehumanized
Separated from her family, sold to a neighboring plantation, her heart cries
Christoria Eve, daughter of Africa . . .
Carry on, brave warrior

Crossing the rough waters of the Atlantic Ocean on board a crowded, unsanitary ship
Inhaling the stench of her fellow third-class passengers for weeks
She holds her children close to protect them from kidnappers and thieves
Arriving, finally, at Ellis Island, standing in the shadow of the Statue of Liberty
She dreams of a new life, sold on the visions of peace, freedom, and opportunity
Homeless, lost, and starting over
Treated like cattle by the port authorities
Elvi, daughter of Finland . . .
Carry on, brave warrior

These are our ancestors, our blood, and our women
Women of our past whose voices are a void within the pages of our history books
Our great-grandmothers, our grandmothers, and our mothers
Mistreated, abused, and courageous
The fiber of our country, America's greatest warrior women
In their honor, we shall make them proud
So I say to you, "Carry on, brave warrior women."

Vulnerability
is a hidden form of
strength.
It's within these delicate moments
that we experience the most growth.

About Fashion Meets Poetry

Fashion Meets Poetry's mission is to create an empowering space for women to embrace the journey of life, the power of story, and the beauty of oneself through poetry, creative self-expression, knowledge and sisterhood.

In our first published poetry book, *Unveiled Beauty*, we help women celebrate their inner and outer beauty and boldly cover sensitive social issues encountered by today's women. Alongside poetry, Fashion Meets Poetry inspires and coaches women through online presence, speaking engagements, and interactive experiences. We accomplish this with our poetry readings, *Fashion Meets Poetry TALKS Business lectures*, and intimate *Unveiled Beauty Circle* discussions. Our goal is to connect with women of all ages at all stages in life with a focus on building confidence, facilitating conversation, learning, self-discovery, and healing.

For more information about **Fashion Meets Poetry TALKS Business** and **Unveiled Beauty Circles**, please check-out our website: www.fashionmeetspoetry.com

Biographies

April Rose Gedney

She tangos with coyotes to the sounds of river currents in unison with her own rhythmic tempo.

Designer. Lover of Gummy Bears. World Traveler. Vintage Enthusiast. Dream Chaser. Entrepreneur.

Favorite Poem: "Set My Heart Free"—It makes me feel alive and rich in love. It puts me in a place of peace and love for myself and God. We have all gone through moments in our lives where we feel scared, alone, and hopeless. I know for me, the day I fully allowed God into my heart and soul, I had never felt more alive, unstoppable, and free.

What does *Unveiled Beauty* mean to you? *Unveiled Beauty* reveals a woman's untold stories—secrets of hardship, pain, love, excitement, passion, growth, and heartbreak. All women harbor these secrets. Some choose to share them while others feel that it's safer to keep them inside. Hopefully, *Unveiled Beauty* will inspire you to open up, knowing you're not judged and not alone. Your friend, aunt, mother, sister, grandmother, and daughter may be able to help you unveil your inner beauty.

Jessica Imse

She whispers to angels with handwritten letters penciled from the etched lines in her soul.

Aspiring Writer. Mother to Four. Dreamer. Old Soul. Chocolate Lover. Quote Junkie. Wife.

Favorite Poem: "Gracefully"—I love its sincerity, simplicity, and bravery. It is a punch in the gut and the tender embrace of a loving friend. It is the weight of truth that simultaneously sinks and releases our insides. I love the dichotomy of pain juxtaposed with freedom. Quite frankly, there are times in my life when I have not been this woman but wish that I had been.

What does *Unveiled Beauty* mean to you? *Unveiled Beauty* is a sensual daydream, a triumphant declaration, an untold whisper. It is a song for every heart, every woman, every passion, and every style. You will find yourself among these pages as well as your mothers, sisters, and friends. We are all universal in our experiences, no matter how different or estranged we may feel from one another.

Autumn Jones

She sails with class through rough oceanic waters in the direction of her determined voice with God's hands at the helm.

California Girl. Straight Shooter. Mother. Lover of Laughter. Wife. Scrapbooker. Cancer Fighter and Survivor.

Favorite Poem: "Hands of Time"—This poem best represents why it has meant so much to be a part of this project. It reflects how we evolve from our experiences and who we will become in the future. The moments that have brought us joy, tears, fear, and courage collectively come together and make us "Older, wiser, and more beautiful than ever before."

What does *Unveiled Beauty* mean to you? *Unveiled Beauty* is our voice, our story that embodies the layers and depth that we have as women, mothers, wives, and friends. It represents how beautiful we are when we stand strong and self-assured. It reflects our beauty when we have lost our way, forgotten who we once were, and are struggling to recognize the person whose reflection we see every day. It exposes to the world how women are so much more than caretakers and emotional support, yet we are so often defined by these roles. Unveiled Beauty celebrates that we are individuals with our own passions, history, interests, experiences, and dreams, and we have a need to be recognized, supported, celebrated, understood . . . unveiled.

Robyn Krenke

She paints hearts with a musical cadence grounded in loyalty as she builds sandcastles in the backyard.

Boy Mom. Green Bay Packer Fan. Music Lover. Crafting Queen. Wife. Cupcake Aficionado.

Favorite Poem: "Our Dance"–This poem is my present, future, and, one day, my past. A relationship between a mother and son is like none other–it is an indescribable bond. Somehow "Our Dance" describes exactly that. It's filled with happiness and sadness as it takes the reader on a journey of motherhood.

What does *Unveiled Beauty* mean to you? *Unveiled Beauty* is our journey. It's the happy, the sad, the moments we cherish and ones we wish to erase. Yet all of those moments are what make us who we are. Everyone will find themselves within these pages and there may be one poem that speaks directly to them, as if it was written about them. It's the unity of women, a sisterhood that welcomes everyone.

Keri Scheibel

She chases fireflies with the northern wind at her back illuminating her jar of hearts.

Runner. Mother of Girls. Diet Coke Addict. Knowledge Seeker. Physical Therapist. Optimist.

Favorite poem: "Thank You Card"—I love its meaning. The woman in this poem is unwavering in friendship and loyalty. She passes no judgment, immovable in her support. Knowing you have a person in your life that will always be there, even if it is just one, is extremely comforting. We can't take friendship, true friendship, for granted.

What does *Unveiled Beauty* mean to you? *Unveiled Beauty* is a story for every woman. It does not judge or discriminate against size, age, race, or religion, but it also does not discriminate against choices we've made. Within these poems, you will find joy, sorrow, and, yes, adversity, but above all, healing.

Reena Vokoun

She dances to the pulse of world beats while balancing on a high wire with arms in outreach from East and West.

Entrepreneur. Fitness Fanatic. Mother of Boys. Loyalist. Positive Thinker. Wife. Dancing with the Stars Fan.

Favorite Poem: "Welcome Home"—The first time I read it, I fell in love with the strength, beauty, vulnerability, and realism it represents. It serves not only to empower women but also to comfort them. We've all been in this woman's shoes, feeling insecure and lost at times but purposeful and fabulous at other times. When I had the honor to model for this poem, I channeled this woman, not only for myself but for all women. Hopefully, in reading it, they will find themselves again and connect with it as deeply as I did.

What does *Unveiled Beauty* mean to you? *Unveiled Beauty* means supporting a dear friend pursue her dream and to be involved in a movement that brings women together in love, strength and community. It's being amongst courageous, unique, and inspiring women, and to have an opportunity to represent the characters in these poems in a creative and heartfelt way.

AUTHOR

Lisa is the founder, poet, and creative director for Fashion Meets Poetry, LLC, and author of her first published poetry book, *Unveiled Beauty*. Before her recent entrepreneurial pursuits, Lisa was the regional director of retail business development at Sanrio, a global company best known for the iconic brand Hello Kitty®. At Sanrio, Lisa was responsible for defining strategic direction, guiding product development, and leading marketing initiatives for Fortune 500 accounts including Target, Kohl's, and Best Buy. Lisa began her career in retail as a buyer at Mervyn's in the San Francisco Bay Area and later as a buyer at Target Corporation, where she spent ten years managing apparel and beauty categories.

Lisa earned her bachelor of business administration degree in marketing from the University of Wisconsin and continues to support the Wisconsin School of Business as a mentor for the Madison Business Mentoring Program, an active member of the Wisconsin Business Alumni Board leading initiatives on the Women In Business Committee, and an Ambassador for the University of Wisconsin *All Ways Forward – Twin Cities Campaign Event*.

Lisa was born in California and raised in a small town in southeastern Wisconsin. She currently resides in Minneapolis, Minnesota, with her husband and two children. Aside from writing and her professional pursuits, she enjoys volunteering at her children's school, attending fashion shows and poetry readings, traveling the world, dining out, supporting local businesses and artists, listening to live music, singing in her car, and dancing in her living room.

WOW!

A shark can hear a fish splashing 820 ft (250 m) away. Human ears can only hear it from about 230 ft (70 m).

Sea birds dive for sardines, because they live just below the surface of the water. Sardines are too small for a shark, but a shark will sometimes try to snap up a bird!

IN THE KNOW

Fisherman in the South Pacific use sounds to hunt sharks. They rattle shells underwater to fake the sounds of splashing fish. Any sharks that come to investigate are killed with a spear.

The Scent of Blood

Sharks have a very strong **sense** of smell. They are especially good at sniffing out the tiniest amounts of blood in water. A shark could smell a teaspoon of blood in a swimming pool.

Sharks search for blood because bleeding animals, such as this ray, cannot swim well enough to escape an attack. This means they make an easy meal for the shark.

When sharks smell blood they become very hungry.

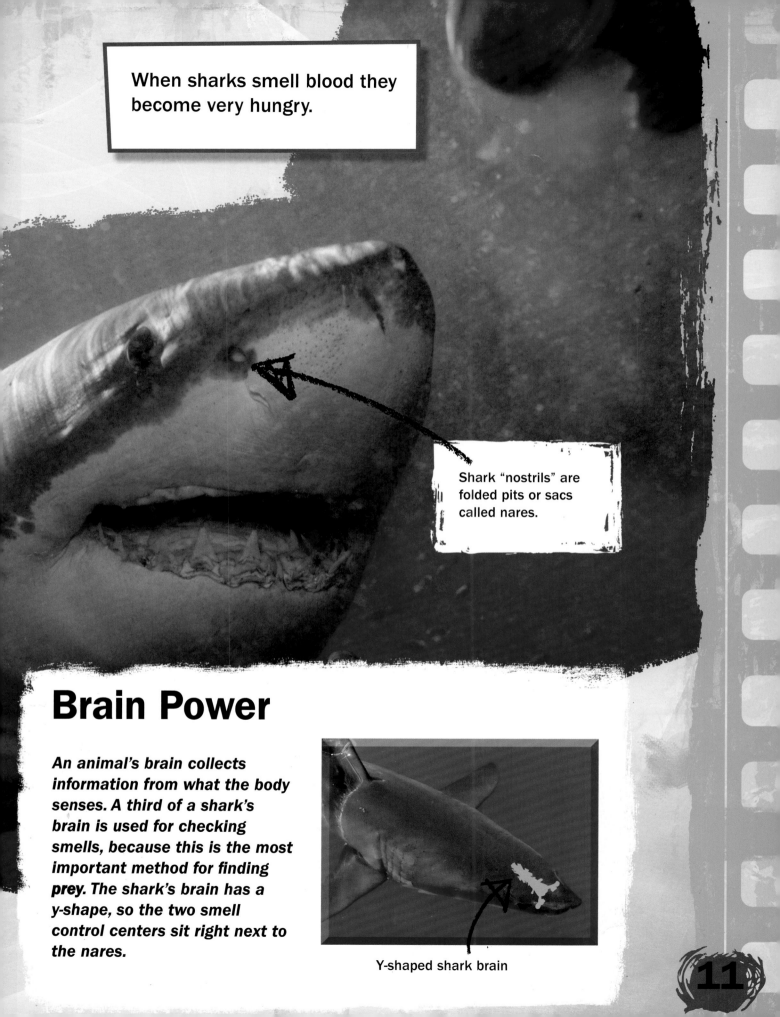

Shark "nostrils" are folded pits or sacs called nares.

Brain Power

*An animal's brain collects information from what the body senses. A third of a shark's brain is used for checking smells, because this is the most important method for finding **prey**. The shark's brain has a y-shape, so the two smell control centers sit right next to the nares.*

Y-shaped shark brain

11

Built to Swim

As a hunter, the shark is always on the move, trying to find prey. Its body is a swimming machine. It can keep going for days without getting tired or out of breath.

Sharks swish their tail to move themselves forward. They use their side fins to steer. Sharks rarely stop moving.

Dorsal fin stops the shark from rolling on its side.

Gill slits

WOW!

A great white shark swims five times faster than a person can.

Side fins work like wings stopping the shark from sinking.

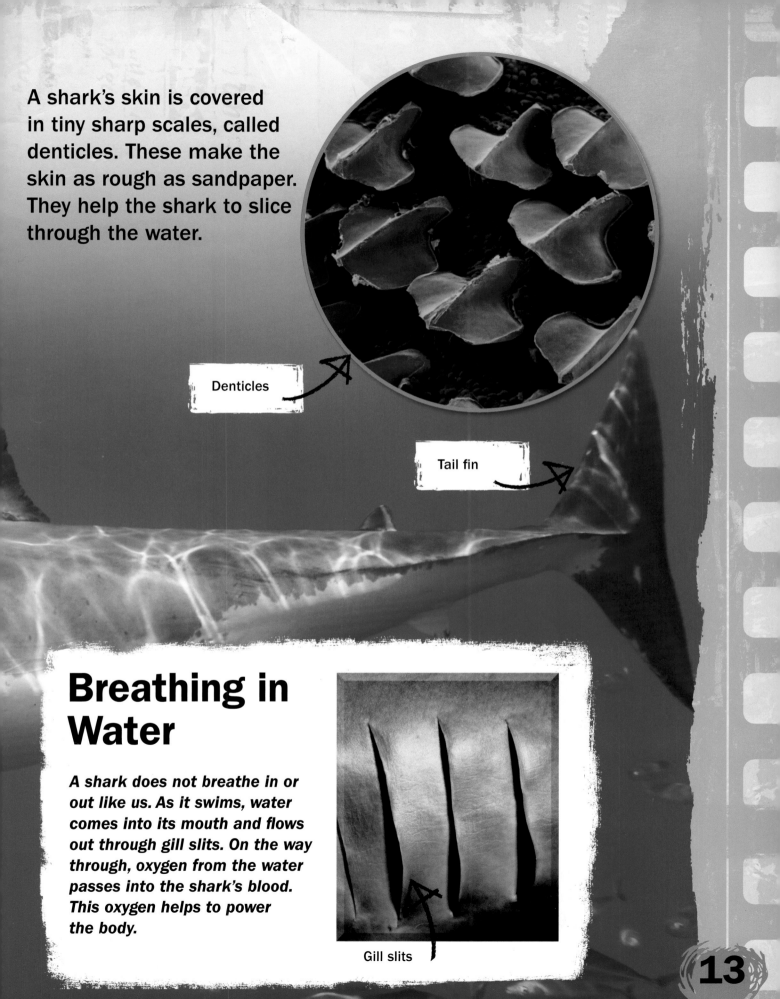

A shark's skin is covered in tiny sharp scales, called denticles. These make the skin as rough as sandpaper. They help the shark to slice through the water.

Denticles

Tail fin

Breathing in Water

A shark does not breathe in or out like us. As it swims, water comes into its mouth and flows out through gill slits. On the way through, oxygen from the water passes into the shark's blood. This oxygen helps to power the body.

Gill slits

Feeling for Prey

Sharks can only see what is in front of them and above them. So they have extra senses to help them pick up what else is around them. They can sense the tiny electrical currents that each living body gives off in the water.

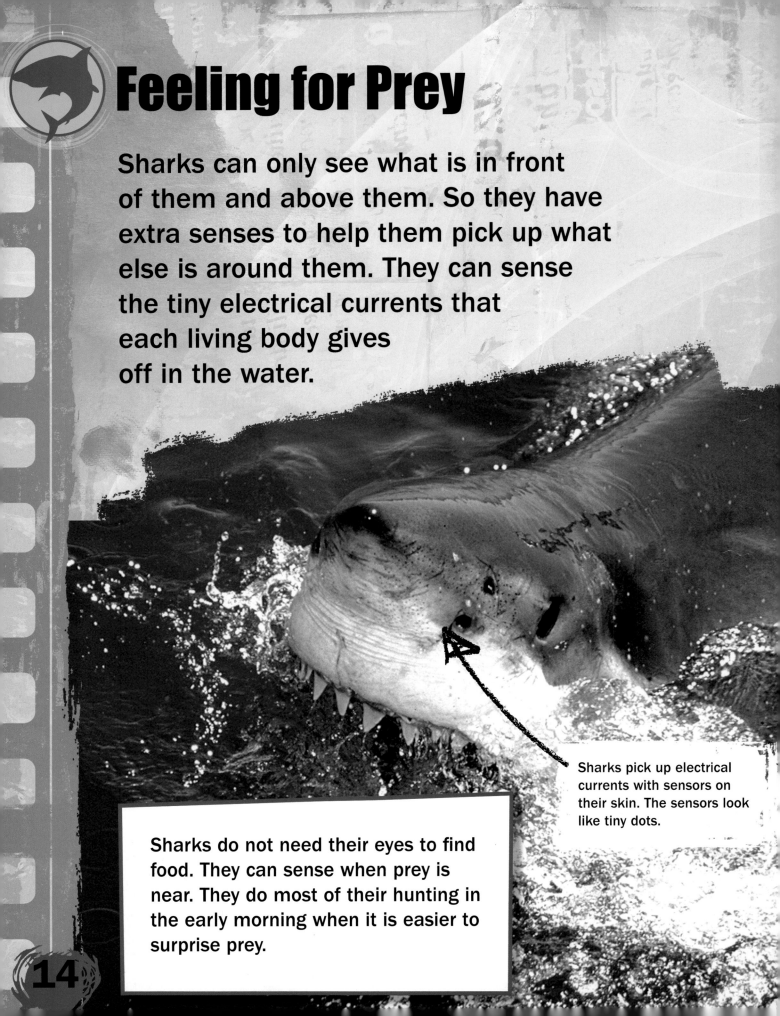

Sharks pick up electrical currents with sensors on their skin. The sensors look like tiny dots.

Sharks do not need their eyes to find food. They can sense when prey is near. They do most of their hunting in the early morning when it is easier to surprise prey.

Sharks can feel the movements of other animals on their skin. When animals move they make tiny currents that the shark can sense.

The great white shark's water current sensors run along the side of its body.

IN THE KNOW

The great white shark's colors make it hard for prey to see it from above and below. From above, its dark top is a similar color to the dark ocean. From below, its white belly blends in with the bright surface of the water.

Friend or Foe?

Sometimes, prey attracts more than one shark. Only one of them will be able to attack and eat the prey. But which one?

When multiple sharks are hunting the same animal, the biggest shark attacks first.

Shark swimming past below.

Talking Like a Shark

When great white sharks meet, they check to see which one is the biggest. They do this in four stages:

1. They swim past each other to compare their length.
2. They have a look from the side to double check.
3. The bigger shark wins, and the smaller one always gets out of its way.
4. The smaller shark hunches its back to signal it has lost.

1.
2.
3.
4.

17

Attack!

Great white sharks have a set way for attacking different prey. Large animals, such as dolphins, or people, are normally attacked from behind. A smaller victim, like a sea lion is hit from below.

Sometimes a shark's attack is so powerful, it jumps clear of the water.

Great whites will strike their prey before biting into it. Great whites roll their eyes back to protect them while they are attacking. This means they cannot actually see what they are biting.

The small sea lion is knocked out by the first bite. It will be too badly injured to swim away.

Top Targets

Great white sharks are not fussy eaters. They will eat all of these animals if they catch them. Each animal has its own tactics to avoid being on the shark's menu:

Sea lions hide in seaweed forests.

Turtles use their shell as armor.

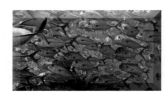
Tuna form large **schools**.

Seabirds fly away when a shark attacks.

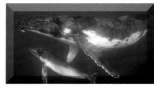
Whale calves stay close to their mom.

Dolphins fight back as a **pod**.

In the Jaws

A great white shark's jaw is one of the deadliest pieces of killing equipment in nature. However, not all shark bites are meant to kill prey.

Great whites like fatty food. They often nudge their prey before attacking. If the prey feels fatty the shark will take a small bite. If the prey is just skin and bones the shark will swim away.

Sharks have two rows of teeth.

IN THE KNOW

Most people who escape from sharks do not escape at all. The shark lets them go because they aren't fatty enough. The shark doesn't like the way people taste.

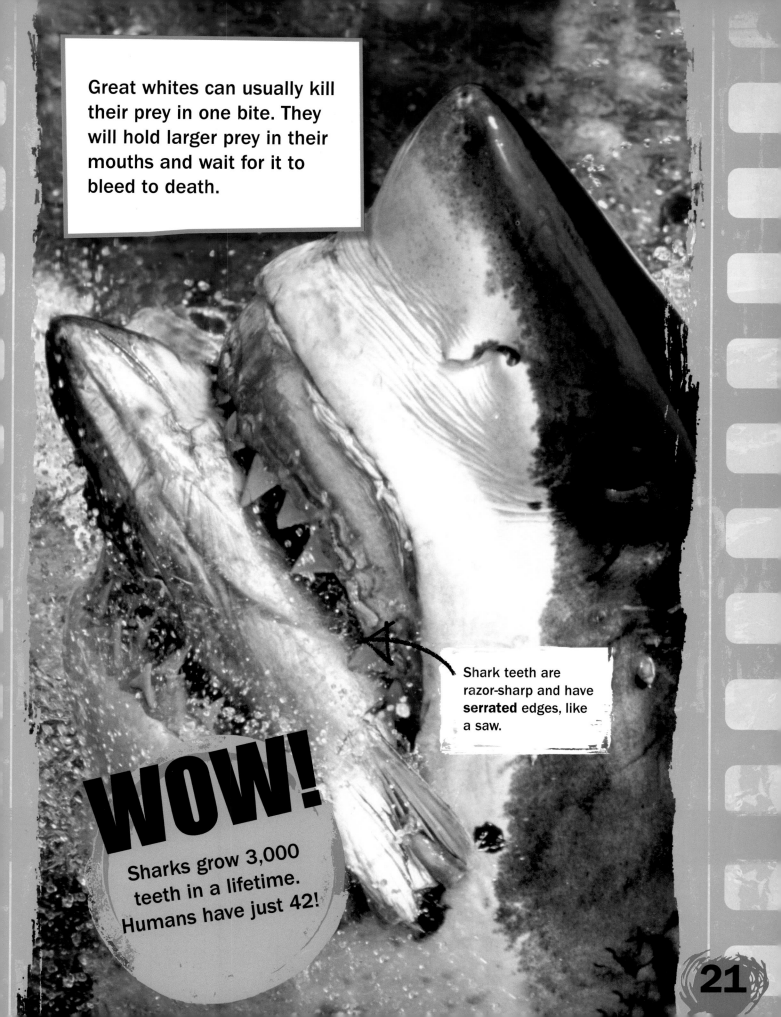

Great whites can usually kill their prey in one bite. They will hold larger prey in their mouths and wait for it to bleed to death.

Shark teeth are razor-sharp and have **serrated** edges, like a saw.

WOW!

Sharks grow 3,000 teeth in a lifetime. Humans have just 42!

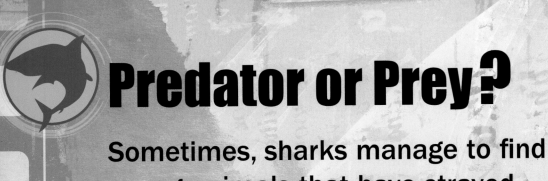

Predator or Prey?

Sometimes, sharks manage to find young animals that have strayed from their parents. Killer whale calves, for example, make a large meal that is easy to catch.

Great white sharks will attack killer whale calves if they are away from their mothers. Great whites will avoid full grown killer whales, since they are bigger and stronger.

Great whites only attack killer whale calves. An adult killer whale is five times heavier than the shark and has an even stronger bite!

Pods of killer whales will attack great whites. They try to spin the great white on its back to confuse it.

When sharks are turned on their back, they fall into a **trance**. In this state, they cannot move and will drown. Some killer whale pods have found this out. They flip great whites on their back and eat their **liver**.

Killer whales try to flip sharks on their back. If the sharks don't get away, they could become prey themselves!

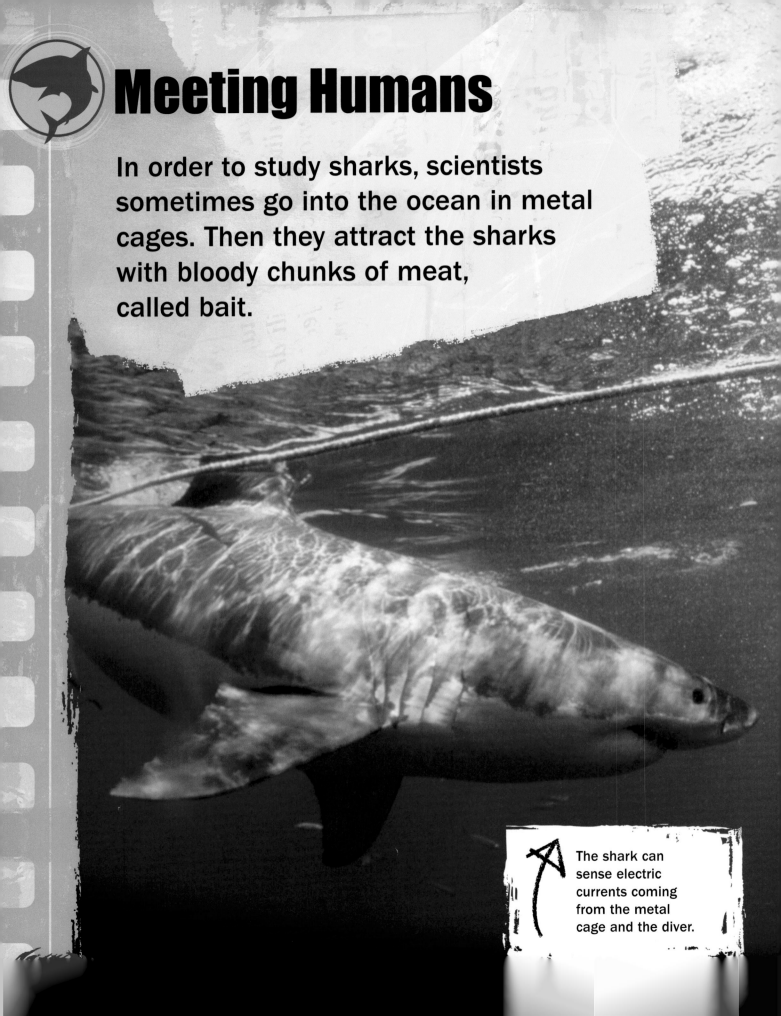

Meeting Humans

In order to study sharks, scientists sometimes go into the ocean in metal cages. Then they attract the sharks with bloody chunks of meat, called bait.

The shark can sense electric currents coming from the metal cage and the diver.

WOW!

Sharks can eat 441 lbs (200 kg) of meat in one meal. That's about 400 times more than a person eats in one meal.

Scientists use long poles to attach a tag to a shark's fin.

IN THE KNOW

Scientists attach tags to sharks. A tag collects information about where the shark goes. After three months, it falls off the shark and floats to the water surface. It then sends its recordings to the scientist.

Underwater camera

Sharks often bite the cages.

Finding a Mate

No person has ever seen a great white being born. We do not even know how the sharks find a mate. Shark tags may tell us more, but until then it remains a mystery.

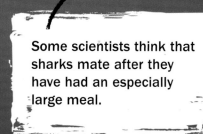

Some scientists think that sharks mate after they have had an especially large meal.

Shark Eggs

Not all types of shark are born. Small sharks hatch out from eggs, sometimes called mermaid's purses. These eggs have squiggly tendrils which tangle with seaweed on the seabed. This is so that the eggs don't get washed away.

Tendrils

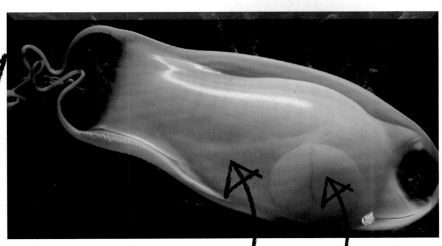

Baby shark growing inside an egg.

Yolk sac

Great whites and many other large sharks first develop in eggs, too. They hatch out of the eggs while they are still inside their mother. Then they grow more and feed on the fatty liquid from the egg's yolk sac.

Newly born lemon shark pup

Yolk sac

Mother

Saving Sharks

Great white sharks are very powerful animals, but they still need our help. No one knows how many great whites are swimming in the ocean. However, people kill so many sharks each year that some types could become **extinct**.

Sharks are often killed in nets. They can get trapped in fishing nets or nets that stop them from getting close to beaches. When they are trapped, they can't move and die.

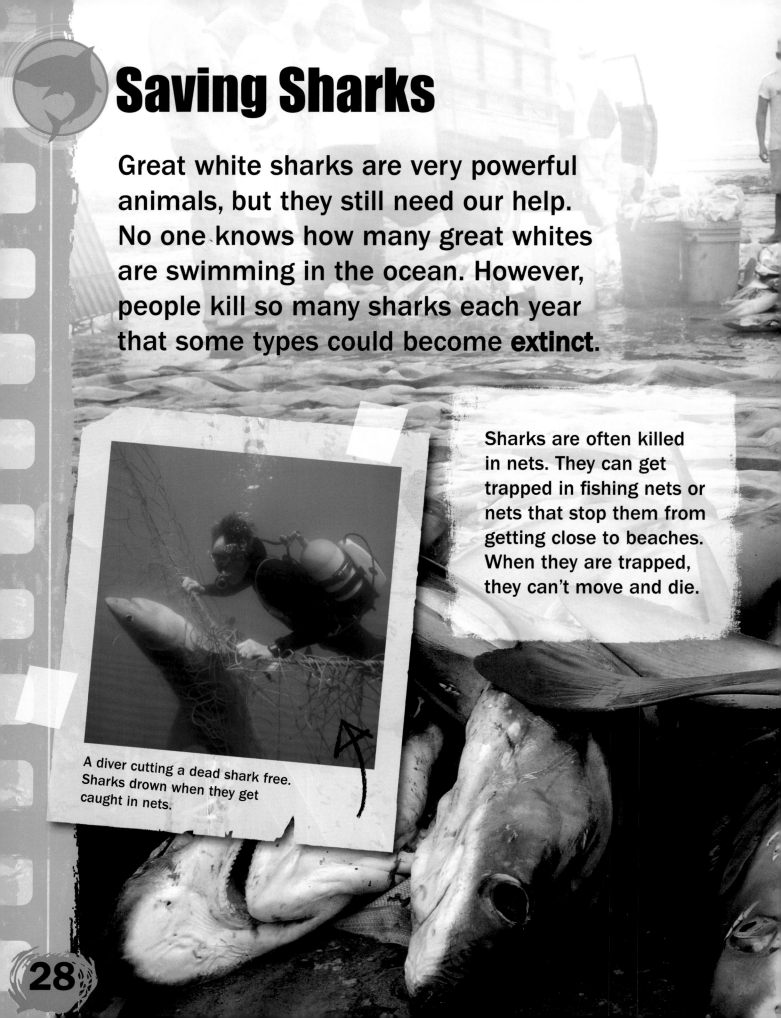

A diver cutting a dead shark free. Sharks drown when they get caught in nets.

Sharks are caught for their meat. The fins are used to make soup.

Sharks kill about six humans each year, but humans kill millions of sharks in that time. Food and sport fishing kills 200,000 sharks every day.

It is against the law to fish for great white sharks. However, **poachers** do kill them and sell their body parts. Some people will pay a lot of money for the tooth or the fin of a great white.

Large great white shark teeth can cost up to $800.

29

QUIZ

1) Sharks have a very poor sense of smell. True or false?

2) How many teeth does a great white grow in its lifetime?

3) How many people are killed by sharks every year?

4) What would happen if a great white shark stopped swimming?

5) A shark's brain is shaped like a "U". True or false?

6) What do sharks breathe with, lungs, or gills?

7) Where are a shark's electricity sensors?

30

Answers:
1) False. Sharks can smell blood from hundreds of metres away.
2) A great white grows about 3,000 teeth in its lifetime.
3) About six people are killed by sharks every year.
4) A shark would sink if it stopped swimming.
5) False. A shark's brain is Y-shaped.
6) A shark breathes with its gills.
7) The shark's electricity sensors are on its snout.

GLOSSARY

dorsal (DOR-sul) To do with the back. The dorsal fin is on a shark's back.

extinct (ik-STINGKT) When all of one type of animal, or species, dies out forever.

liver (LIH-ver) The largest organ inside the body.

migration (my-GRAY-shun) When animals make long journeys to find food, mates or a better place to live. The journey is always a round trip because the animals eventually return to where they started.

oxygen (OK-sih-jen) A gas mixed into air and water that is used by a living thing to release energy from food to power the body.

pectoral (PEK-tuh-rul) To do with the chest area.

pelvic (PEL-vihk) To do with the lower body area.

poacher (POH-cher) A hunter who breaks the law by killing animals that are protected by hunting bans.

pod (POD) A group of dolphins or whales.

predator (PREH-duh-ter) An animal that hunts for other animals and then kills them for food. Great whites are the world's biggest predatory shark.

prey (PRAY) Animals that are hunted and killed for food by predators.

scales (SKAYLZ) Waterproof plates that cover a shark's body.

school (SKOOL) A group of fish.

sense (SENS) To hear, feel, see, taste or smell something.

serrated (ser-AYT-ed) Something is serrated when it is covered in a zigzag of spikes and is used for cutting.

trance (TRANS) A relaxed state when the animal is awake but might behave like it is asleep.

Index

blood 10, 11
brain 11

denticles 13
dolphin 18, 19
dorsal fin 4, 12
dwarf lanternshark 4

egg 6, 27
electrical currents 14, 24

gills 5, 12, 13

jaw 20, 21

killer whale 22, 23

lemon shark 27

mating 26, 27
migration 6

nares 11

pectoral fin 5
pelvic fin 4
people 18, 24, 25, 26, 28
poachers 29
predator 4, 22–23
prey 11, 12, 14, 15, 16, 18,
  20, 21, 22, 23
pup 6, 7, 26, 27

sardine 9
scientists 24, 25, 26
sea bird 9, 19
sea lion 16, 18, 19
sense of smell 10, 11
sensors 14, 15

teeth 20, 21, 29
tuna 19
turtle 19

whale 19
whale shark 4, 5

Web Sites

Due to the changing nature of Internet links, PowerKids Press has developed an online list of Web sites related to the subject of this book. This site is updated regularly. Please use this link to access the list:

powerkidslinks.com/insti/shark/